Jin checks in the bag.
It has a lot in it.

Chun will go to the shops.
Chun will get a box of fish.

To the Shops

By Stephen Rickard

ılished in 2026 by
rwood House Press
44 Clinton Street
falo, NY 14224

ıted in the United States of America

Library of Congress Cataloging-in-Publication Data:
Names: Rickard, Stephen, 1957-, author.
Title: To the shops ; Jets / written by Stephen Rickard.
Description: Buffalo, NY : Norwood House Press, 2026. | Series: Phonics all-stars: phase 3 |
Identifiers: ISBN 9781978578111 (pbk.) | ISBN 9781978578128 (library bound) | ISBN 9781978578135 (ebook)
Subjects: LCSH: Reading–Phonetic method–Juvenile literature. | English language–Phonetics–Juvenile literature. | Shopping–Juvenile literature. | Jet planes–Juvenile literature.
Classification: LCC LB1573.3 R534 2026 | DDC 372.465–dc23

CPSIA compliance information: Batch #CW26NHP: For further information contact Norwood House Press at 1-800-237-9932.

Jin is at the shops.

Jin has lots of bags.

Will Chun go to
the shops on a yak?

Nen will go to the shops.
Nen will get a dish of nuts.

It is a lot of nuts.

Nen can get a mug of nuts as well.

Jad will go to the shops.

Jad will get a rug. His wish is to get a red rug.

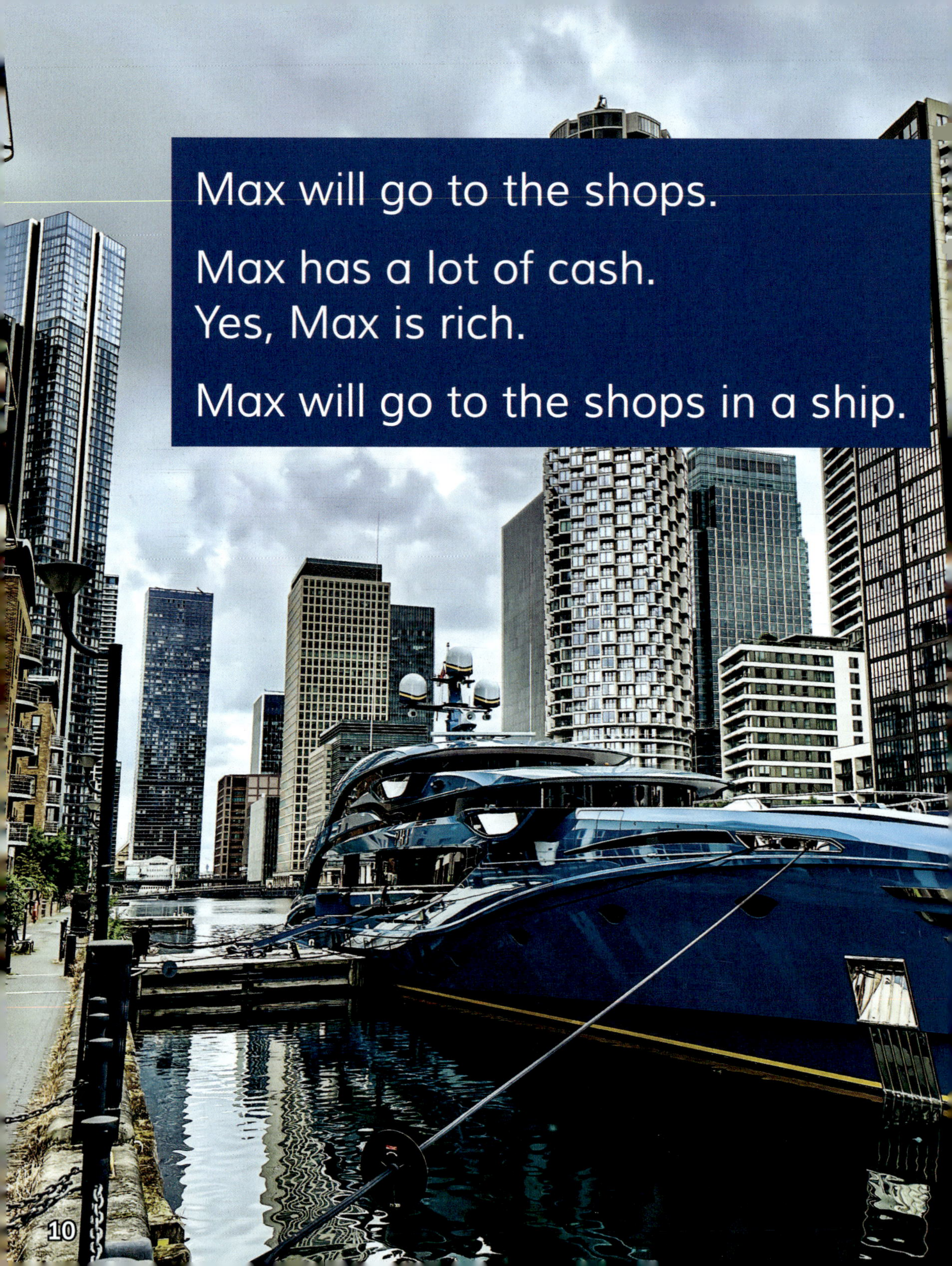

Max will go to the shops.

Max has a lot of cash.
Yes, Max is rich.

Max will go to the shops in a ship.

At the shops, Max will get a jet.

I will go to the shops.
I will get a jet as well.

But the jet I will get is
not as big.

Jets

By Stephen Rickard

This is a jet.
It is quick.

This man sits in the jet.
He gets such a buzz.

This is a big jet.
It is quick as well.

The wing is long and thin.
It lets the jet be quick.

Lots of men sit in this jet.
The men will not get a buzz.

Jam the men in the jet!

This is not fun.

The jet zips up in a rush.

This man checks the jet.
Will he fix it?

No, he will not fix it. ***She*** will.
She will fix the wing.

This jet is on a ship.
The ship has lots of jets on it.

This man has a fun job. On the deck, he tells the jet to go.

This is not a jet.